A DIFFERENTIATED APPROACH TO THE COMMON CORE

How do I help a broad range of learners succeed with challenging curriculum?

Carol Ann **TOMLINSON** | Marcia B. **IMBEAU**

 Alexandria, VA USA

ASCD | arias™

Website: www.ascd.org
E-mail: books@ascd.org

www.ascdarias.org

PAPERBACK ISBN: 978-1-4166-1979-6   ASCD product #SF114076

Also available as an e-book (see Books in Print for the ISBNs).

Library of Congress Cataloging-in-Publication Data
Tomlinson, Carol A.
  A differentiated approach to the Common Core : how do I help a broad range of learners succeed with challenging curriculum? / Carol Ann Tomlinson and Marcia B. Imbeau.
    pages cm
  Includes bibliographical references.
  ISBN 978-1-4166-1979-6 (pbk. : alk. paper) 1. Effective teaching--United States. 2. Individualized instruction--United States. 3. Mixed ability grouping in education--United States. 4. Education--Curricula--Standards--United States. I. Imbeau, Marcia B. II. Title.
  LB2805.T63 2014
  379.1'58--dc23
                                2014024912

_____

21 20 19 18 17 16 15 14   1 2 3 4 5 6 7 8 9 10

A DIFFERENTIATED APPROACH TO THE COMMON CORE

How do I help a broad range of learners succeed with challenging curriculum?

Want to earn a free ASCD Arias e-book?
Your opinion counts! Please take 2–3 minutes to give
us your feedback on this publication. All survey
respondents will be entered into a drawing to
win an ASCD Arias e-book.

Please visit
www.ascd.org/ariasfeedback

Thank you!

The Opportunity and the Challenge

The Common Core State Standards provide teachers with an opportunity and a challenge. Taught effectively, the Common Core standards encourage students to *understand* what they are learning (rather than largely memorize and repeat information) and to *apply* and *transfer* what they learn. The result would be "deep learning," which is much more durable and useful than rote learning or "surface learning." That's the opportunity. The challenge is that the Common Core demands this level of learning from more than just the "smart" or "advanced" kids. It requires virtually all learners to think in complex and creative ways and be able to use what they learn in contexts beyond those practiced in class.

While our best knowledge of teaching and learning indicates this expectation is entirely appropriate, for many of us, thinking about how to teach complex content in a classroom where student needs and readiness levels vary considerably is unfamiliar territory. The goal of this brief publication is to provide a framework for developing curriculum and planning instruction for academically diverse student populations in Common Core classrooms or, for that matter, in any classroom that calls on all students to master intellectually rigorous standards. To that end, we offer an eight-step process for creating differentiated lessons based on Common

Core standards and then delivering this instruction in a way that supports the successful understanding of a broad range of learners.

All of the steps are discussed at an introductory level, as our goal in this publication is to launch a pathway to learning, not to complete it. To learn more about each of the eight steps, please refer to the list of resources available online at www.ascd.org/ASCD/pdf/books/DICOMMCORE.pdf. Due to space restriction, we've also chosen to illustrate the principles in action with a few examples that should be clear to teachers in all grades and content areas.

Step 1: Planning to "Teach Up"

A teacher who believes that dynamic curriculum enlivens learning for all students and who is genuinely optimistic about all students' prospects for success enters the planning process in a very different place than a teacher who believes that curriculum is a textbook or a list of standards to be covered and only some students have the capacity to succeed academically. The former, optimistic approach is what we call "teaching up."

"Teaching up" is rooted in what Carol Dweck (2006) labels a "growth mindset"—the belief that it is not so much an intelligence quotient that determines success in school as it is a person's willingness to work hard and persist in the face of difficulty and the presence of a support system that both encourages and informs the hard work. Teachers with growth mindsets believe that the brain is malleable and that the more we teach students as though they are smart, the more likely they are to become smart. Teachers who work from a growth mindset envision student capacity as something like an iceberg: a great deal of potential is hidden from our view at any given time. The best teaching stems from the intent to teach to the unseen as well as to the visible in order to bring to the surface additional possibilities.

"Teaching up" means planning instruction for the broadest possible range of learners. It means aiming high and then building scaffolding that helps all students reach those heights, including the students who may not have seen themselves as capable of making the climb. It is not a casual statement that "all kids can learn" but rather an enacted commitment to working with all students—step by step and regardless of what their entry point into a discipline, unit, or topic may be—in a way that makes their growth evident to them and fuels their motivation to keep moving forward.

"Teaching up" begins with the teacher asking, "What is the most thought-provoking, interesting, and engaging lesson (or unit) I can design to ensure that students will want to invest energy in complex questions, address significant issues, and master skills necessary for success with critical content?" Later in the design process, that question is followed by another: "How can I plan time, space, resources, and other elements to ensure that students with varied needs will have the opportunity to move ahead in their own learning and work as a contributing part of the class as a whole?" It does not suggest creating "harder" curriculum but rather creating intellectually rigorous curriculum that stretches students' thinking. "Hard" curriculum is taxing, burdensome, and demotivating; "rigorous" curriculum is energizing, enlivening, and motivating.

"Teaching up" is a state of mind that can be learned. It permeates all aspects of curricular and instructional planning as well as the teaching/learning process. Each of the remaining seven steps we'll look at will be significantly shaped by the degree to which the teacher believes that compelling curriculum can build young minds, believes in the potential of every student to work intelligently and hard in pursuit of success, and embraces the responsibility of crafting curriculum and instruction that will maximize the success of each learner in the class.

Step 2: Developing Learning Targets

Key to creating challenging curriculum based on Common Core standards is understanding the role of standards in curriculum and what it means to use standards to engage student thinking and promote understanding. While a set of standards is *important* in designing curriculum, a set of standards is *not* a curriculum. A curriculum is—or ought to be—something far richer, more compelling, and more meaningful than any list of standards can be. It is a plan to help students make sense of, relate meaningfully to, and apply the wisdom of an academic discipline such as math, literature, science, social studies, art, music, and so on. Curriculum should help students to make meaning of the world around them and continually envision their potential roles in that world. Correctly used, standards contribute significantly to curriculum, but they are no more the curriculum itself than a bag of groceries is a four-star meal.

When selecting the standards that will become key ingredients in a curriculum, a teacher can begin with a single standard or cluster of standards and ask, for example, "How can this/these standard(s) help my students understand folk tales, fairy tales, myths, and legends as literature passed down through generations?" Another option is to begin with the question "Why do people in all times and places share stories?" and then think about which standards will contribute most effectively to students' exploration of that question as it relates to folk tales, fairy tales, legends, and myths. It arguably keeps us closest to the power of what we teach if we begin with the discipline or with the topic that's an exemplar of the discipline, and weave in standards that are a good fit. In either case, it's important to be thoughtful and purposeful in selecting standards that will contribute most significantly to student understanding of critical content rather than simply teaching a set of standards as standalones. There are three guidelines for the selection process.

Determine the essential meaning of what you will teach. Although "What is the point of this topic or lesson or unit?" seems like a straightforward question to ask, it can be anything but easy to answer. For example, if students in a math class study a unit on graphs and simply learn to create several kinds of graphs, there is little take-away meaning. On the other hand, if their teacher explains they will be working with graphs as one tool for expressing mathematical relationships alongside other tools like words, equations, and tables, the students are much more likely to be able to use graphs purposefully. In this way, teaching graphs as tools to show relationships (rather than simply "teaching graphs") helps students make meaning of graphs—and of mathematics. Understood fully, a particular topic, lesson, or unit can provide a gateway to understanding something bigger than itself. Effective teaching is not about covering standards but about using standards as one tool to help students understand the world around them and themselves in that world.

Select standards most likely to help students make meaning of content. When planning a unit, look for clusters of standards that can work together to help students develop a fuller understanding of the content in question. Although it sometimes makes good sense to teach a single standard, it never make sense, in terms of student learning, to teach a decontextualized list of standards one at a time. Look for connections among standards that will help students learn both more broadly and more efficiently.

For example, Mrs. Martin, a 1st grade teacher, selected four standards for use in a three-week unit. One lesson near the end of the unit incorporates the story "The Garden" from *Frog and Toad Together*, and she will prompt students to think about how the story relates to their lives and experiences. At that point, the students will use writing—first to retell events in the story in sequence and then to share their opinions about patience, a key theme in the story. Here are the Common Core standards she chose:

- Describe characters, settings and events in a story using details (RL.1.3).
- Retell stories (including key details) and demonstrate understanding of their central message or lesson (RL.1.2).
- Write narratives in which they recount two or more appropriately sequenced events, include some details regarding what happened, use temporal words to signal event order, and provide some sense of closure (W.1.3).
- Write opinion pieces in which they introduce a topic they are writing about, state an opinion, supply a reason for the opinion, and provide some sense of closure (W.1.1).

In Mrs. Martin's plan, these four standards will work together to help students explore details in the story, understand messages in the story, retell the story in sequence to demonstrate temporal understanding, and share an opinion about a central message in the story. At the early stages of the unit, the students will work with these standards singly and in combination in a variety of contexts.

Determine the KUDs for the unit or lesson. "KUD" is shorthand for what a student should **K**now, **U**nderstand, and be able to **D**o as the result of a segment of learning. KUDs are the *learning targets,* the critical outcomes of the segment of study. They can also be called *essential knowledge, essential understandings,* or *essential skills* (Wiggins & McTighe, 2005). Clear KUDs are critical to aligning goals, formative assessment practices, instructional plans, and summative assessments. They serve as thinking and planning "lenses" to focus teacher and student efforts throughout the learning process.

Knowledge (Ks) includes the names, dates, people, places, lists of items, processes, and so on that learners must acquire in order to build a foundation for the learning ahead. **Understandings (Us)** are statements of truth that reveal to learners the meaning of what they are learning, how the topic or content or discipline really works, why it matters, how it relates to other topics or content, and what makes it tick. They are "ahas," overtures to insight. Understandings should be written as complete sentences and phrased so that they could follow the words "I want my students to understand *that . . .*" rather than *what,* or *why,* or how, because those lead-ins don't set up the understanding as a clearly articulated truth. So, for example, a U for a high school history class might be (I want my students to understand that) *Revolution is often preceded by evolution.* Finally, **Dos (Ds)** are skills—the verbs or verb phrases that delineate what actions students should be able to take as a result of learning.

For students to have full power of learning, they must build knowledge (acquire Ks), make sense of what they learn (develop Us), and be able to use what they learn (execute Ds). All standards—Common Core and otherwise—are phrased as Ks, Us, and Ds. In fact, because the Common Core emphasizes outcomes, all Common Core standards are written as Ds. To ensure that students are learning in the multiple dimensions necessary for ownership of the Common Core's complex content, instructional designers need to identify the unstated but frequently implied Ks and Us that are embedded in the standards. This is what we mean when we talk about "unpacking" the standards: examining them and rephrasing them in a way that clarifies both the explicit and implicit KUDs.

The following is an example of the KUDs derived from a 7th grade Common Core standard for reading literature. Note that these KUDs incorporate both implicit and explicit knowledge, understandings, and skills derived from unpacking the standard. They also incorporate additional Ks, Us, and Ds that stem from the teacher's knowledge of her students' needs, interests, and experiences, along with her sense of how she can help her students connect with the standard as something relevant to and important for them.

Common Core Standard: Analyze how particular elements of a story or drama interact (e.g., how setting shapes characters or plot) (RL.7.3).

Know:

—Elements of fiction (plot, setting, character, theme)

—Analysis, evidence, interaction, supporting a position

Understand:

—Elements in our lives affect us and affect one another. The people we associate with help shape us—and we help shape them.

—Time of day, weather, where we are, and the music we hear all impact our mood, thoughts, and actions.

—The "themes" of our lives that most strongly represent who we are and what we stand for shape our thoughts, lives, and actions.

—Authors use the elements of fiction in purposeful ways to guide readers' thinking.

—Stories are representations of life and, in that way, act like our lives do.

—Each element in a story shapes every other element in the story.

Do:

—Recognize the elements in a story.

—Analyze how the elements interact—and why.

—Provide evidence from the story to support their explanation.

Similarly, unpacking the four Common Core standards selected by Mrs. Martin for a unit that incorporates "The Garden" (see p. 6) might yield this set of KUDs:

Know:

—Topic, opinion, reason, conclusion/ending, events, events in the correct order, detail, temporal words

Understand:

—It often takes hard work over a long time to learn or do something new.

—If we're not patient when we try to learn or do something new, we get frustrated or unhappy.

—Being patient with ourselves helps us persist with things that are challenging.

—Authors often tell stories to help us understand ourselves and our world.

Do:

—Tell, draw, or write what happened in "The Garden."

—Share (tell, write, draw) a narrative about a time they were impatient because something seemed too hard or took too long.

—Share (tell, write, draw) how they acted when something seemed too hard or took too long.

—Share (tell, write, draw) why patience could make them stick with challenges and make them proud of themselves.

—Write an opinion piece that states an opinion about whether or not patience helps people be better learners.

In both examples, notice that most of the KUDs stem from the standards that are the unit's foundation, either explicitly or implicitly. However, both teachers have also added "ingredients" that link the standards with their students' experiences as a way to ensure clarity and relevance and promote understanding. In other words, these teachers are doing a lot more than simply "covering" the standards.

Creating a set of strong unit learning targets/KUDs, which are then subdivided into KUDs for individual lessons, is neither a quick process nor a static one. Teachers who are willing to think about ideas and edit their insights will fare much better than those who seek easy or formulaic pathways to learning targets. In addition, a teacher who carefully observes how students engage with the unit's learning targets will be well positioned to clarify, refine, and extend learning targets for units and lessons over time.

Step 3: Designing Lessons

Moving from KUDs to the specifics of a unit or lesson plan calls on teachers to once again think about their students, considering ways the curriculum might by shaped to respond to students' varying experiences, cultures, languages, interests, and so on. Unsurprisingly, it is possible to design a unit on a given topic and set of KUDs in an infinite number of ways. The goal is to generate a plan that will connect *this* content with *these* learners.

To create durable plans that are also pliable and responsive, it's wise to reflect on the learner variance that recurs from year to year, such as weak readers, students missing important prerequisite knowledge, English language learners, advanced learners, students who approach learning in a variety of ways, and students with weak academic vocabularies. With an awareness of how learners may differ, you can build in mechanisms to attend to such differences: small-group instruction, additional practice, varied modes of presentation, multiple ways of demonstrating knowledge, materials at varied reading levels and in different languages, and so on.

Embracing "pliable planning" means using three questions to guide the design process: (1) How can I "package" and "deliver" the KUDs for *my* students so that they will engage with the KUDs and can make sense of and use what they learn? (2) In what order will it make most sense for *these* students to encounter, practice, and apply what they are learning? (3) How long is it reasonable to spend on each segment of the teaching/learning sequence, knowing that there must be some built-in flexibility?

These questions are recursive. For example, a high school teacher may decide that a truly engaging way for her students to use geometric methods to solve a design problem to satisfy physical constraints or minimize cost (HSG.MG.A.3) would be to have them design a skateboard park for the school's campus, following prescribed safety guidelines and budgetary limits. However, if the teacher can only allot eight class periods to this unit, and the project would require at least four of these periods, the teacher will likely need to consider another plan. In other words, lesson design requires us to consider "packaging," sequence, and time more or less simultaneously.

Strong curriculum nearly always tells a story. There is a sequence of ideas—the "characters" or "players"—and a sense of introducing, complicating, and then resolving an issue or an unknown. There is a setting or context, and a theme, punch line, or big idea that will be revealed. Consciously or unconsciously, powerful teachers weave stories through their curriculum design and help students be participants in those stories, because this is what makes the content relevant to students' experiences and makes it understanding focused, thought provoking, and memorable.

Now let's look at a few examples of how teachers moved from KUDs to challenging curriculum. We'll begin with Mrs. Navin, a kindergarten teacher. She developed a set of KUDs for a math unit focused on counting, which represents one of the two Common Core–identified "critical areas" for kindergarten mathematics: that students (1) use numbers to represent quantities and (2) solve quantitative problems. Here are the three Common Core topic clusters (each encompassing individual mathematical content standards) and three mathematical practices that are central to the unit, along with the KUDs that Mrs. Navin generated:

Common Core Standards for Mathematical Content and Mathematical Practice

—Students know number names and the count sequence (K.CC.A).

—Students count to tell the number of objects (K.CC.B).

—Students compare numbers (K.CC.C).

—Students make sense of problems and persevere in solving them (MP1).

—Students construct viable arguments and critique the reasoning of others (MP3).

—Students attend to precision (MP6).

Know:

—Counting numbers and names (cardinal) from 1–100

—Ordinal numbers and names

—More than, less than, counting, ordering, plan, explain thinking

Understand:

—We can use numbers to solve problems.

—We can talk about how we are thinking.

—We can make a plan to help ourselves count and solve problems.

Do:

—Count with cardinal and ordinal numbers.

—Show results.

—Explain thinking.

—Respond to plans and thinking of others.

—Develop and explain a plan for counting.

As is often the case in kindergarten, counting and conversations about counting are pervasive in Mrs. Navin's classroom. Students count out loud as a class and in small instructional groups, talk about counting and how it can help them, and practice counting-related skills individually or with a partner. In the lesson we'll look at, Mrs. Navin asked students to use counting to figure out how many students were in class that day. Later in the lesson, Mrs. Navin followed up with small-group conversations that drew on both the KUDs and the mathematical practices. Because of where this lesson fell in the unit's sequence, it included many, but not all, of the unit's KUDs:

Know:

—Counting numbers and names (cardinal)

—More than, less than, counting, ordering, plan, explain thinking

Understand:

—We can use numbers to solve problems.

—We can talk about what we are thinking.

—We can make a plan to help ourselves count and solve problems.

Do:

—Count with cardinal numbers.

—Show results.

—Explain thinking.

—Respond to plans and thinking of others.

—Develop and explain a plan for counting.

Although the students received versions of the task that were the best match for their current levels of proficiency with counting, all versions of the task focused on the same KUDs.

Because Mrs. Navin knew that her young learners were in very different places on a continuum of counting proficiency, she planned at the outset for a lesson that would (1) be center-based, so that students could work with the task at different times; (2) use tasks at different levels of complexity to create appropriate levels of challenge; (3) extend over several days to allow her to discuss the completed tasks with groups of students; and (4) allow for students to return to the center to refine their approaches. In Step 6, we'll share the details of Mrs. Navin's differentiated lesson.

Our second example comes from the classroom of Ms. Askins, the 7th grade ELA teacher who created KUDs based on the Common Core reading standard (RL.7.3) that asks students to analyze the interaction among elements in a short story or drama (see Step 2, p. 9). While KUDs stemming explicitly or implicitly from the standard were clear to her, she also felt that many of her students would be less than captivated if she simply asked them to describe how the elements interact in a story of her choice—or even in a story of their choice. In moving from a set of KUDs to curriculum design, her goal was to create an introductory lesson that would help the students relate to the idea of interaction of elements. Therefore, she added the first three understandings listed (see p. 10) to the understanding that is explicit in the standard ("Each element in a story shapes every other element in the story") and an understanding that is implicit in the standard ("Authors use the elements of fiction in purposeful ways to guide readers' thinking").

Ms. Askins decided that before she would begin to teach about and have students work with the knowledge and skills targeted in the unit's KUDs, she would lead them in a substantial conversation about how the elements work in their lives by asking questions like "Who here is a morning person and who is a night owl?" "What happens if you stay up too late or get up too early?" and "Tell us about a time when someone you associated with made you a better person."

Ms. Askins knew that the concept of *theme* in literature is abstract and often difficult for teens to grasp, and that a student who considers, "What themes do I see in my own life?" has opened the door to a more solid understanding of themes in literature. Once her 7th graders could explain how elements in their own lives interacted, Ms. Askins would help them see that stories are just representations of lives and, as such, they aren't so difficult to analyze and explain. She concluded that spending two class periods on this analogy would make the remainder of a two-week unit much more effective. She also decided that this was an instance when beginning a unit with a careful explanation of essential understandings would help her "tell the story" of interaction of elements in literature much more powerfully than if she began with reviewing or teaching knowledge and skills.

There are no recipes to follow in moving from KUDs or learning targets to designing units and lessons that aim to ensure student success in mastering the KUDs. That progression is creative. It means keeping a constant eye on the KUDs to ensure tight and consistent alignment with plans. It also requires a willingness to think flexibly and reflectively about the meaning of the content, the needs of students, and the myriad ways the two might be connected.

Step 4: Assessing Formatively

It's easy and familiar to create a sequence of lesson plans designating what will take place on Monday, what will follow on Tuesday, and so on. Too often, however, those plans focus on what the teachers and students will *do* in a prescribed time frame rather than on what will be *learned.* Doing is no guarantee of learning—especially when the teacher does lots of the doing!

Powerful curriculum design includes two frequently overlooked elements critical to student learning: (1) persistent formative assessment and (2) built-in instructional time for teachers to attend to student needs that formative assessment results have revealed.

Formative assessment is sometimes called assessment *for* learning, whereas summative assessment is called assessment *of* learning. Said another way, summative assessment is intended to see if the students "got it," and formative assessment is intended to help ensure that the students "are getting it." Any activity, quiz, or assignment used for formative purposes should result in clear, specific feedback that lets each student know what's going well at this specific point in the learning cycle and what could be done next in order to keep moving forward.

The names of the two categories of tools for formative assessment indicate when in the teaching/learning process they are used. *Pre-assessments* are used prior to beginning a unit of study (or very shortly after the unit begins, if it is highly likely that students have had no prior access to the content). *Ongoing assessments* are used throughout the learning cycle to monitor development of student knowledge, understanding, and skill. Appropriate use of formative assessment results in flexible instructional grouping based on evolving student learning rather than "fixed" groupings based on teacher perceptions of student "ability." Here are the characteristics of effective tools for formative assessment:

- They are tightly aligned with the unit or lesson KUDs. Pre-assessments typically look at student status with a *unit's* key goals. Ongoing assessments typically look at student status with a *lesson's* key goals. Pre-assessments are also useful in checking student readiness with prerequisite skills.

- They are designed so that students can demonstrate understanding, application, or transfer rather than just recall knowledge or perform skills in isolation.

- They are generally created to sample student learning rather than assess it thoroughly. Neither pre-assessments nor ongoing assessments should take a lot of time to develop, administer, or analyze.

- They are rarely graded. Pre-assessments, in fact, are never graded, as they precede instruction on and practice with the material being pre-assessed. Ongoing assessments should generally not be graded, because students are still practicing their developing knowledge, understanding, and skill. When we grade practice, we discourage the kind of intellectual engagement necessary for understanding.

- They result in high-quality teacher feedback to students.

- They often include an opportunity for students to analyze their own formative assessment results or those of peers, using clear guidelines, rubrics, or

checklists, which helps to further their academic
growth and confidence as learners.

- They lead directly to an adjustment in instructional
plans to better attend to the varied statuses of students.

It's difficult to overstate the importance of aligning formative assessment plans with unit or lesson KUDs. Effective
teaching and learning are built on (1) achieving clarity about
what students are expected to know, understand, and be
able to do as a result of a segment of learning; (2) designing
learning experiences that absolutely mirror those KUDs; (3)
monitoring the same KUDs throughout the learning process
with ongoing assessments; (4) responding to students' needs
relative to the KUDs as revealed by the formative measures;
and (5) creating summative assessments that are a direct
measure of the KUDs to give a sound measure of student
proficiency with the KUDs. Any mismatches among learning targets, instruction, assessment, or reporting are costly
in terms of student success.

The many useful formats for pre- and ongoing assessment include brief quizzes, exit cards, Frayer diagrams,
journal entries, annotated diagrams, teacher use of obser-
vational checklists, and teacher-student interviews. In fact,
almost any work students do can serve as a tool for formative
assessment, as long as the assignment is aligned with KUDs
and the teacher reviews the work with an eye to improving
instruction based on what the outcomes reveal.

As with other aspects of designing challenging curriculum for a broad group of learners, formative assessment

should be planned with student differences in mind. A teacher might ask questions like "Are there students who lack context for this assessment prompt?" "Would it be wise to build in support for reading?" "Could the vocabulary used in this set of directions get in the way of student understanding?" and "Would it support student success to provide more than one way to express learning?"

For the first of two examples of teachers using formative assessment to guide instruction and monitor student progress, we'll consider Mrs. Martin's process for her 1st grade unit on describing story events, retelling events in sequence, using temporal words to link events, and writing opinion pieces. When designing her unit, she decided to use a teacher-student interview as a pre-assessment. Over a period of several days, she met with each student for about five minutes. Using a checklist to guide her thinking about student responses, she asked all learners to do the same three things. First, she asked them to arrange some simple sketches in an order that tells a story and to share with her the story in the pictures. This gave her a sense of the individual students' readiness to arrange and retell events in sequence and the degree to which they were incorporating temporal words into their expression. Second, she asked them to describe a place shown in one of the sketches and a character who appeared in several of the sketches. This gave her a sense of the individual students' comfort with description and the kind of vocabulary they used in that process. Finally, she asked them to tell her what, in their opinion, was the best part of school and why they thought so. This exchange helped Mrs. Martin develop a sense of the students' understanding of what an opinion is and what it means to give reasons for an opinion.

Ms. Askins, the 7th grade English language arts teacher, created a four-question pre-assessment for the units she built around a Common Core standard on the interaction of elements in short stories and dramas:

(1) Explain in words or words and images how you think our lives are like the lives of characters in a story or a movie or a play. (2) What are the elements of fiction? Please define or describe the elements you list. (3) How would you explain to a 4th grader what you do when you analyze something? (4) What do you think is the most important theme in your life? What theme does the best job of capturing who you are and what you stand for?

Looking back at the unit KUDs on page 10, you can see that this pre-assessment aligns well with them and would give a snapshot of student status with some key Ks (elements of fiction, theme), a key D (analyze), and a central U (stories are representations of life and, in that way, act like our lives do). This pre-assessment would also help to prepare the students to participate in the important analogy discussion that anchors the unit.

Ms. Askins decided to differentiate her pre-assessment. In consideration of the English language learners in her classes and several students who were struggling with writing for a variety of other reasons, she provided the class the option, in question 1, of expressing their thinking in writing *or* in annotated images. When working with particular individuals or small groups, she prompted students to state their answer out loud, knowing that what they were able to put down on paper might not be a full reflection of their thinking. Some students had the option of typing their answers into a document on the computer or using a recorder to capture their spoken responses.

It's not imperative to differentiate assessments, but one hallmark of a good assessment is that it enables students to show full knowledge, understanding, and skill. If an aspect of the assessment (such as vocabulary, demands for writing, or time limitations) constrict students' opportunity to share what they know, the assessment becomes less effective. What we *can't* differentiate in an assessment (making an exception for some students who have Individualized Education Plans indicating different learning goals) are the KUDs that the assessment measures.

Throughout this unit on interactions among elements in short stories and plays, Ms. Askins also used a variety of ongoing assessments to monitor her students' developing knowledge, understanding, and skill. For example, at one point in the unit sequence, students read a short story and then worked in pairs, quads, and as a whole class to decide on its theme, the most insightful ways to state the theme, and how the author used the elements of fiction to develop the theme. Following that three-day learning experience, Ms. Askins was ready to sample her students' learning. After having the entire class watch a brief video clip that told a story, she distributed the following prompt:

> Please select **one** of the following options to demonstrate your understanding of the ideas we've worked with over the last two class periods. Your answer should be brief but clear and showcase your most important thinking. *Option 1:* State what you believe is theme of the video clip we just watched. Then explain how the author used characterization, setting, theme, and plot to help viewers think about that theme. *Option 2:* Draw a diagram that shows how the various elements of a short story affect one another—and how they work together to create a theme or main idea. Label your diagram so its meaning will be clear to viewers.

Again, looking at the unit KUDs, it's clear that the assessment aligns with the portion of the KUDs targeted in the three-day lesson and with the learning experience that students had. Students were allowed to select the option that best spotlighted their thinking, and Ms. Askins's decision to use a video as the text allowed her better access to the developing understanding of students who struggled with reading or simply related better to the visual presentation.

Note that Ms. Askins did not use pre-assessment or ongoing assessment with an eye to markedly change the "narrative" of her unit or alter the unit or lesson KUDs. Rather, she gathered data that helped her arrange time, resources, and support in a way that maximized her students' forward momentum with content important for their continuing development as learners.

Step 5: Refining Instruction

If the definition of formative assessment includes use of resulting data to improve the teaching/learning process, then it's important to consider how a teacher might move from creating and administering pre-assessments and ongoing assessments to refining instructional plans based on what the assessments reveal about student learning. Analyzing formative assessment results is different than the typical grading process. The goal of examining a piece of student work is not to be able to say, "You got 78 percent of these questions correct," or "Based on our rubric, your work is a B+" but rather to answer this very important question: "What approach to tomorrow's lesson will help me best serve each of my students?" Answering this question is a three-step process.

Recall the targets of the assessment. Without clarity on what you are trying to measure, you can't abstract instructionally useful information from formative assessment responses. Was the assessment's goal to measure Ks, Us, Ds, or some combination—and which ones? Are you looking for student status in regard to particular prerequisite knowledge, understanding, and skill? If so, which? Do you hope to discover who can provide correct answers—or who can also apply or transfer what they've learned?

Determine patterns in student responses. This step associates the performance of clusters of students with the specific learning targets. You identify, for example, that these students can provide correct information but are not able to apply it. These other students lack fundamental understanding of two key ideas, and this third group of students demonstrates a basic understanding but cannot support their thinking with illustrations.

Decide what comes next. The goal is not to generate individualized lesson plans but rather to find patterns in student responses and then cluster students for practice targeted at their next steps in learning. The progress they make in these small groups allows for and leads to additional whole-class work that is meaningful and productive.

Let's return to Mrs. Martin's classroom (see Step 4, p. 23) to look at how assessment analysis can shape instructional decision making. As a pre-assessment, she interviewed her students one on one, guided by a checklist that helped her identify which sorts of practice and support would be most useful to them, both individually and as a whole class, as they began their work. In analyzing the checklists, she found a wide range of variance in the sequencing task, especially related to the use and range of temporal vocabulary words. Most students could describe the place in the sketches with appropriate words, but their vocabulary sophistication varied considerably. A number of students struggled to describe the character in a way that demonstrated understanding of the story. Finally, while most students could give an opinion about the best part of school, many had difficulty providing clear reasons for their choices.

Mrs. Martin used the patterns she found in the pre-assessment to refine her whole-class instructional plans and some individual and small-group plans. In working with the whole group, she spent less time than she had projected on general description and dug a bit deeper on descriptions beyond easily identifiable physical or visible traits. Prior to this whole-group work, she engaged students struggling with temporal words in a teacher-led, small-group session on this topic, having reasoned that a preview would put the students in this group, several of whom were English language learners, in a much better position to participate in and understand the whole-class work. She also decided to vary some of the learning center's vocabulary tasks by word complexity but still kept all the tasks focused on "words that help us put things in order" and "words that help us describe."

Now let's consider the instructional refinements Mr. Gorman made while he and his 6th grade social studies students were engaged in a month-long unit called "Exploration of the New World." In the early days of the unit, students examined knowledge about the geographical world at the start of the time period, the role of science in limiting or supporting exploration, costs incurred in exploration, funding of exploration, reasons for exploring, exploration routes, varied perspectives about costs and benefits of exploration, and so on. Then, midway through the unit, students worked in quads to create annotated route maps for a number of explorers. Each group drew the route of a particular explorer, annotating it by answering several teacher-provided questions (e.g., "When/where did the journey begin and end?" "What was a likely high point of the exploration and why?" "What was a low point and why?"). Students shared their work with two other quads and used two additional teacher-provided questions to compare and contrast the journeys of the three explorers.

Mr. Gorman moved continually among the groups, asking questions of both individuals and groups related to how they were working and what they were understanding. Carrying a clipboard with a class list of students, he made note of who seemed comfortable using texts to glean information and who was having a more difficult time. He also noted individuals who could not respond to his questions at a baseline level of comprehension. Then, at the conclusion of the two-day lesson, he asked the students to complete the following 3-2-1 Card as an additional means of formative assessment:

> Please provide the . . . **3** most important pieces of advice explorers in this time period would have passed on to explorers who came later . . . the **2** different perspectives about or opinions on exploration by groups or individuals who lived during the time of European exploration . . . the **1** idea you'll take away from mapping an explorer's route.

Mr. Gorman's review of student responses, combined with the notes he took as the students worked on the route mapping assignment, helped him understand varied degrees of challenge that would be appropriate in an upcoming lesson. He was then able to envision a task at two levels of complexity and design the supports that would allow his broad range of learners to engage successfully with intellectually rigorous work. We'll look at the process for doing this—and the specifics of what Mr. Gorman did—next, in Step 6.

Step 6: Scaffolding and Extending Challenge

This step calls on teachers to use both general and specific knowledge of students to provide the support these students need to accomplish tasks that may initially appear beyond their reach. Effective challenge for any student stretches the student beyond his or her comfort zone and therefore requires teacher support, peer support, or both.

Here a teacher might continue to ask general questions about teaching with student variance in mind: "How can I build in extra time for practice with current or prerequisite content?" "How can I best extend learning for students who show early success?" "When will it work for me to meet with small groups so that everyone gets my attention in this context?" But this is also the time when a teacher must make plans for specific learners and clusters of learners: "Given the reading range and English fluency of these learners, which materials will be best for this lesson?" "How can I make connections between the understandings in *this* unit and the interests of the students in *this* class?" "How can I 'chunk' this presentation so that several students who have difficulty listening can stay engaged with the ideas?" "What questions can I ask in the discussion that will challenge the students who already have a deep understanding of the content?" In other words, the goal is to combine your best sense of the necessary knowledge, understandings, and skills with your best knowledge of your specific learners and, in doing so, connect content and kids.

Recall that the Common Core and differentiation have the shared goal of "teaching up," otherwise known as providing intellectually challenging, understanding-focused curriculum for the broadest possible range of learners. This means all students should experience lessons that satisfy the criteria noted in Step 3—lessons that look like what educators have long thought of as "curriculum for the smart kids." To succeed with this kind of curriculum, some students will need scaffolding some of the time. For some students, some of the time, even this complex curriculum will not provide enough of a challenge to trigger individual academic growth. They will need the challenge extended, which means they, too, will require thoughtful support in order to stretch to the new level of expectations.

In the pedagogical sense, **scaffolding** refers to any temporary support that will help students achieve both better understanding of content and independence as a learner. It can include instructional strategies, tools, materials, additional teaching, checklists, models, diagrams, organizers, and other mechanisms that will help a student move from a particular point of entry into the unit or lesson to a desired point of achievement. While we think of scaffolding as important for students who struggle with learning, in truth, it's something all students need when expectations for their work are beyond their current points of performance. Scaffolding is about addressing factors that would otherwise keep students from focusing on the essential KUDs of a unit or lesson. It is not giving a student less work related to what he or she doesn't understand. It is not watering down instruction or having students focus only on information and skills until they are "ready" to take on understanding and application. Here are a few examples of effective scaffolding:

- Providing reading material (including directions and assessments) at a student's reading level or in a language the student can read and understand
- Pre-teaching academic vocabulary
- Providing instructions in multiple forms (orally, with visual icons, and in writing)
- Providing models of competent student work slightly beyond a student's current performance level
- Using small-group instruction to provide targeted instruction or practice
- Providing graphic organizers or templates
- Distributing timelines for work completion

- Giving explicit feedback on the next steps in learning based on formative assessment information
- Connecting content with student interests
- Using technology to support student reading, writing, speaking, hearing, or movement
- Breaking work into smaller parts
- Ensuring planned opportunities for needed practice
- Using peer brainstorming groups to prime thinking and planning
- Offering multiple modes of activities or assessments
- Helping students set, monitor, and adjust goals
- Providing opportunity and support for revising work

Extending challenge for a student who demonstrates high competence with current Ks, Us, or Ds means trying to stretch the student's experiences with the content through breadth, depth, or complexity in learning. While moving ahead to the next step with content that's organized in a linear way (e.g., math, world languages) can be useful to some advanced learners, the goal of extending student learning is to provide opportunities to think more extensively, look at content through varied lenses, apply or transfer content into more complex and uncertain contexts, and examine big ideas or understandings as they relate to different disciplines. Extension means mental extension, not workload extension. Approaches to extending curriculum include the following:

- Providing advanced resources
- Assigning tasks that are more complex, abstract, open-ended, or multifaceted

- Assigning tasks that require deeper or wider thinking, reading, research, application, or questioning
- Offering feedback that focuses students on the depth, breadth, and quality of their ideas related to the unit's understandings
- Providing advanced criteria for success and models at a high level of excellence
- Asking students to use multiple concepts, multiple skills, or unknown skills to address problems or issues
- Assigning tasks that ask students to probe multiple meanings or examine perspectives unlike their own
- Building on students' interests as a means of deepening understanding
- Asking students to articulate and support multiple (and contradictory) perspectives
- Allowing a greater degree of student choice related to content, process, and product to support developing independence
- Offering coaching for quality and growth beyond the student's current level of performance

Let's look at how two of the teachers we've spotlighted scaffolded and extended the challenging curriculum they teach, beginning with Mrs. Navin. The Common Core standards and KUDs of her counting-focused kindergarten unit can be found on pages 15–17. In one learning center experience spread out over part of three class days, Mrs. Navin's students made plans to count how many students were in their class, carried out these plans, discussed their plans with the teacher and a small group of peers, and then revised and re-executed their plans twice.

Mrs. Navin assigned students to a color-coded task at the learning center, basing these assignments on both careful informal assessment and the formative assessment data she had collected over the prior two weeks. All worked with the core goals of counting to solve problems, making a viable plan to solve problems, persisting in solving problems, sharing plans with peers, and critiquing the plans of peers. Figure 1 shows the three sets of directions for the three groups.

FIGURE 1: **Directions for a Differentiated Kindergarten Learning Center Task**

Orange Group	Blue Group	Yellow Group
• Find a way to count and show how many people are in our class.	• Find a way to count and show how many people are in our class.	• Find a way to count and show how many boys are in our class today.
• How many are absent today?	• Be ready to tell how you got your answer.	• How many boys are absent today?
• How many are here today?		• How many girls are here today?
• Be ready to tell how you know.		• How many girls are absent today?
		• Be ready to prove you are right.

Mrs. Navin met with students in each group before they began their center work to be sure they understood the task—making a plan, carrying out the plan, and sharing the plan. A picture chart reminding her students of these steps was posted at each center. After students completed their task, she again met with the three groups separately and posed questions about the nature of the students' plans, how they carried them out, whose counts were higher (or lower) than other counts, why these answers varied, whether they should vary, and how and why the students might do the job a different way.

While students in all three groups did work that was explicitly aligned with the KUDs, Mrs. Navin scaffolded the work of the blue group by reducing the number of variables they had to deal with, and she extended the work of the yellow group by increasing the number of variables they had to deal with and asking them to work for accuracy. She also used both pre-task and post-task small-group discussions to support success and to stretch thinking by adjusting questions based on current student readiness and responses.

Now we'll turn to Mr. Gorman, whose 6th graders were studying European exploration of the New World (see Step 5, pp. 29–31). Here are the Common Core standards that were the foundation for the unit and the KUDs for one lesson.

Common Core Standards:

—Integrate content presented in different media or formats to develop a coherent understanding of a topic or issue (RI.6.7).

—Write arguments to support claims with clear reasons and relevant information (W.6.1).

—Show how two or more sources address similar themes or topics to build knowledge (CCRA.R.9).

Know:

—Names and key biographical information about two New World Explorers

—Key events of contribution

Understand:

—Exploration involves risk, costs and benefits, success, and failure.

Do:

—Show how two or more resources can be used to build knowledge on a topic or idea.

—Develop an argument that supports claims with clear reasoning and relevant evidence.

In the lesson, the students' job was to use a variety of print and online resources to expand their understanding of two explorers and build an argument, based on the information they found, that "their" explorers did or did not support the lesson's key understanding (see the U above). Mr. Gorman began by developing a task for students whom he knew were strong thinkers, had a good grasp of the content, and read with solid comprehension. He then created a more scaffolded version of the same task that retains the KUDs but makes them more accessible to more students by providing prepared sets of resources and product options, stating the key understanding to illustrate in the product, and using more straightforward language. See Figure 2 for the abbreviated directions for both versions of the task.

FIGURE 2: **Directions for a 6th Grade Differentiated Research Task**

Version 1	**Version 2**
Using reliable and defensible sources, develop a way to show how your two New World explorers were paradoxes. Include and go beyond the unit principles in building a case that they do *or* do not support the key understanding for today's lesson. Be sure to integrate information from several sources to support your case.	Using the provided lists of resources and product options, illustrate how your two New World explorers took chances, experienced success and failure, and brought about both positive and negative change. Provide proof/evidence from your reading. Using what you learn from varied sources, build a case that these explorers either do or do not support the key understanding we've discussed for today's lesson.

Mr. Gorman might have scaffolded Version 2 further by providing resources boxes with relevant materials in them, bookmarking key passages in sources, having students plan in teacher-led start-up groups, permitting students to read or write in their first language, providing graphic organizers with prompts to guide information gathering and synthesis, giving directions one step at a time, having students check in with the teacher after each step, and so on.

These examples show teachers beginning with a lesson idea that is engaging and likely to promote understanding.

From there, the teachers add a variety of scaffolds and extensions to ensure individual growth toward and, when possible, beyond the complex learning targets.

Step 7: Assessing Summatively

Summative assessment is assessment *of* learning, and it comes after students have had appropriate time to both encounter and make sense of new knowledge, understanding, and skill, and therefore, at a point when it is reasonable to expect them to demonstrate proficiency with the content: at the end of each "chunk" or segment of a unit, at the end of the unit, at the end of a marking period, at the midpoint of a course or school year, or at the end of a course or school year.

Summative assessments typically are graded and take one of three forms: (1) traditional paper-and-pencil tests that are close-ended; (2) performance tasks, which include open-ended problems to address; and (3) products, which are longer-term student creations requiring them to apply the unit's KUDs to problems, issues, or an area of interest. Although there are exceptions, traditional paper-and-pencil tests are generally better suited to assessing knowledge and skill, and performance assessments and products are generally better suited to assessing understanding and transfer. For that reason, all three types of summative assessments, when well-constructed, can play a useful role in measuring student outcomes.

Effective summative assessments share the following characteristics:

- They tightly align with the unit KUDs. They measure student proficiency with the knowledge, understandings, and skills designated as essential at the outset of the unit.
- They emphasize student understanding—not solely or even largely information and skill. They call on students to apply and transfer what they have learned.
- They are designed in a way that "opens up" rather than constricts student opportunity to demonstrate learning. This may include variation in wording, the option to use technology for writing, and the choice of using different modes of expression. Again, what must remain constant are the KUDs that the assessment measures.

Arguably, the prime hallmark of an effective summative assessment is the first one listed: its alignment with the unit's designated learning targets (KUDs). This underscores the degree to which successful teaching and learning depends on destination clarity. Everything else that follows—planning how to teach up, assessing formatively, modifying instruction to increase student success—is dependent on knowing the destination and careful planning to ensure that everyone arrives there. Straightforward as that sounds, it's easy to stray. One common pitfall is the practice of designing summative assessments just before it's time to administer them. While that practice sounds logical, it predictably results in an assessment focused on "what we just covered" rather than the initial learning targets.

As a way to avoid this "drift," Wiggins and McTighe (2005) propose a three-stage process they call "backward design." In Stage 1 of the backward design process, curriculum designers carefully specify standards relevant to the unit under construction and list essential knowledge, essential understandings, and essential skills derived from unpacking the standards. (This is our Step 2.) In Stage 2 of backward design, curriculum designers lay out all of the summative assessments that will be used in the unit before instructional planning ever begins. The goal of this early-stage design of summative assessments is to ensure their alignment with essential learning targets before anything else can intervene. In Stage 3 of backward design (also our Step 3), curriculum designers construct teaching/learning experiences that, in a stepwise fashion, guide students to achieve the learning targets.

"Backward design" is eminently wise practice. We are strong advocates of its architecture. Summative assessments are measures of student success with significant portions of the teaching/learning process. They are also measures of teacher success. The more thoughtful we are with designing that process, and the more reflective we are in carrying it out, the more successful we will be in guiding our students to learning success.

Step 8: Leading and Managing for Success with Challenge

For many beginning teachers, the most unsettling part of their work is "managing" students. The prospect of shepherding 25, 35, or more young learners through a class period or school day is, at the very least, daunting—and sometimes terrifying. And so, we develop management patterns designed to "control" the students and minimize the chance for chaos to ensue. We ask them to begin working at the same moment, to stop their work at the same time, to stand and sit in unison, to pass in their papers simultaneously, and so on. In time, most teachers become proficient with this approach to "managing" student behavior and classroom routines as though everyone were essentially alike. And, in time, we come to speak of our students as a single unit: "They were restless today." "They don't like it when we do drills." "Third period's projects were really great."

It's highly unlikely that every student understands, misunderstands, likes, dislikes, is restless, created a terrific project, and so on, but it's easier to think of "the class" or "the students" than to think about X number of individuals. Nonetheless, that habit constricts both teaching and learning. In virtually every class, some students have knowledge gaps, some are past ready to move ahead, some have great difficulty sitting still, and some need extra teacher time for a re-explanation of what didn't make sense yesterday or because they were absent yesterday.

As we've noted earlier, the Common Core requires a very broad range of students to become thinkers and problem solvers, and differentiation is what allows us to address the varied learning needs of those students. However, neither complex thinking nor attention to student differences can happen well or consistently in rigidly managed classrooms. At the same time, classroom chaos is never acceptable, and we know that effective classroom management is a strong contributor to student achievement (Hattie, 2009).

Experts tell us that there are two kinds of "orderly" classroom environments—orderly restrictive environments and orderly enabling environments. *Orderly restrictive environments* run smoothly but with tightly managed routines and relatively few instructional approaches in evidence. In these classrooms, student thinking is minimized because the "messiness" of debating ideas, making mistakes, and dealing with the inevitable uncertainty that comes with complex thought isn't possible. *Orderly enabling environments* also run smoothly. They have a looser, but not loose, structure and give evidence of a wider range of routines and instructional approaches. These orderly enabling classrooms are the ones in which inquiry-oriented, thought-intensive work is likely to take place (Darling-Hammond & Bransford, 2007; Educational Research Service, 1992). They exhibit a sound balance between the structures and routines necessary for predictability and the flexibility necessary to attend to both thinking processes and student learning differences.

The final step in helping the broadest range of students succeed with challenging curriculum focuses on working with students to implement an orderly, flexible classroom necessary for both complex thought and differentiation. This two-part process calls on teachers to first lead students to understand and contribute to a classroom designed to work from varied entry points toward increasing competence and confidence as learners and thinkers. Then it requires the teacher to work with students to create and implement routines that allow student-centered instruction and balance the need for predictability and flexibility. In other words, the teacher first *leads* students and then *manages* details.

Leadership includes ensuring that students understand and can relate to the reasons a differentiated classroom can be beneficial to each of them and to the group as a whole, talking through how this sort of classroom is both like and different from other classrooms they've been part of, figuring out what sorts of rules or guidelines will work best in such a classroom, thinking about the roles of teacher and students in the classroom, defining what "fair" will mean, clarifying the nature and role of quality work, and so on.

Managing routines includes knowing how to start and stop a class smoothly, when and how to move around the room to complete tasks effectively without disturbing others, how to turn in completed assignments, how to get help when the teacher is working with small groups or individuals, what to do when assignments are completed, how to manage noise levels, and so on.

Classrooms in which teacher and students work together to honor learning differences and establish a balance between structure and flexibility support the interrelated goals of the Common Core and differentiation. Figure 3 capsules two days in Mrs. Navin's kindergarten class during the unit on counting and illustrates curriculum that is both orderly (with clear KUDs derived from Common Core standards and aligned with instruction and formative assessment) and flexible (with whole-class, individual, and small-group instruction, and tasks differentiated by readiness, interest, and learning profile) and delivered in an environment designed to provide both stability and flexibility.

FIGURE 3: **Differentiated Instructional Plans for a Kindergarten Math Unit**

Whole-Class Activities	Differentiated Activities
Tuesday Review of cardinal numbers Calendar math emphasizing cardinal numbers	
	Ordering events using cardinal numbers—four readiness-based groups
	Group 1: Ordering pictures
	Group 2: Ordering pictures with sentences
	Group 3: Telling a story in steps
	Group 4 (Teacher Guided): Telling a story with Spanish and English cardinal numbers

Whole-Class Activities	Differentiated Activities
Wednesday Review of what it means to make a plan to solve a problem Group planning to figure out how to count the number of students who wore coats to school today	
	Students rotate through • Teacher-led, small-group work with calendar math, based on formative observations • Readiness-based calendar math work at student tables • Center-based work on using counting to solve a problem

Concluding Thoughts

This publication has provided a compact examination of an approach to planning curriculum and instruction based on the Common Core or other rigorous standards that is designed to ensure that the broadest range of students not only be able to access the highest-quality learning opportunities we can create but also receive the support they need to grow through mastery of important content.

The process is not a simple or mechanical one. It requires a great deal of study, thought, self-reflection, and persistence from teachers. That's as it should be. The approach we have outlined is the essence of teaching—something that challenges us and enriches us, both as professionals and as human beings. Welcoming the challenge professionalizes us as educators, and it revitalizes the possibility of schools as places that enliven young people, helping each of them build a life of promise.

To give your feedback on this publication and be entered into a drawing for a free ASCD Arias e-book, please visit
www.ascd.org/ariasfeedback

ENCORE

A CHECKLIST FOR REFLECTING ON THE EIGHT STEPS FOR DIFFERENTIATING COMMON CORE INSTRUCTION

Response Key:

+ I do this consistently while continuing growth in this area.

→ I'm going in the right direction here, but I know I need to improve.

? My work in this area is questionable and I need to grow significantly.

Step 1: Planning to "Teach Up" as a Catalyst for Challenge and Success

___ I see human differences as positive and enriching in the classroom.

___ I believe virtually all students have the capacity to succeed academically.

___ I accept responsibility for each student's growth and success.

___ I work to know and respond to each student's culture, interests, and perspectives.

___ I continually study my content to understand it for meaning and relevance.

___ I continually study my students to understand them as learners.

___ I exhibit high expectations and high support for each student.

Step 2: Developing Learning Targets for Challenge and Success

___ I think deeply about the meaning and relevance of the content I teach.

___ I select and group standards to help students learn dynamic content.

___ I unpack standards to determine their explicit and implicit knowledge, understandings, and skills.

___ I add additional KUDs to represent important meaning in the disciplines I teach.

___ I think about the students I'll teach as I write KUDs.

Step 3: Designing Lessons for Challenge and Success

___ I use the narrative/story in what I teach to help students make meaning.

___ I ensure that lessons tightly align with the KUDs I have written.

___ I consider the students I'll teach as I develop lessons.

___ I build flexibility into lesson plans that allows attention to student needs.

___ I package and deliver KUDs for student engagement and understanding.

___ I order content in the way I feel will best support student understanding.

Step 4: Assessing Formatively to Guide Instruction for Challenge and Success

___ I regularly use pre-assessments and ongoing assessments to understand student proximity to the KUDs.

___ I ensure that formative assessment aligns with KUDs.

___ I emphasize student understanding in formative assessment questions.

___ I create formative assessment measures that sample rather than exhaustively measure student progress.

___ I use varied forms of formative assessment.

___ I consider differentiating formative assessment tools so students have the best opportunity to demonstrate their learning.

___ I give students feedback on formative assessment results to guide their work.

Step 5: Refining Instruction for Challenge and Success

___ I keep associated KUDs in mind as I study formative assessment results.

___ I study student responses to find patterns of strength and need related to the KUDs.

___ I decide best instructional responses to address the patterns I find.

Step 6: Scaffolding and Extending Challenge

___ I continually think about the evolving status of each of my students as they master the KUDs.

___ I ensure that teaching/learning plans are tightly aligned with the KUDs.

___ I ensure that teaching/learning plans are engaging and focus students on understanding, application, and transfer of the KUDs.

___ I use a wide range of scaffolding in teaching/learning to ensure access to robust curriculum for students still working to master the KUDs.

___ I use a wide range of extensions in teaching/learning to ensure depth and breadth of learning growth with content for students who demonstrate mastery of the KUDs.

Step 7: Assessing Summatively to Determine Success with Challenge

___ I ensure that summative assessments align tightly with the KUDs.

___ I emphasize student understanding rather than only/largely information and skill in summative assessments.

___ I use varied forms of summative assessment.

___ I design summative assessments to ensure opportunity for students to demonstrate fully what they have learned.

Step 8: Leading and Managing for Success with Challenge

___ I actively plan time and space to address students' varied learning needs.

___ I trust in my students' capacity to work with increasing independence and productivity.

___ I lead students to be my partners in creating a classroom that works for everyone.

___ I manage classroom routines and procedures to allow attention to students' varied learning needs.

References

Darling-Hammond, L., & Bransford, J. (2007). *Preparing teachers for a changing world: What teachers should learn and be able to do.* San Francisco: Jossey-Bass.

Dweck, C. (2006). *Mindset: The new psychology of teaching.* New York: Random House.

Educational Research Service. (1992). *Academic challenge for children of poverty: The summary report* (ERS Item #171). Arlington, VA: Author.

Hattie, J. (2009). *Visible learning: A synthesis of over 800 meta-analyses relating to achievement.* New York: Routledge.

Wiggins, G., & McTighe, J. (2005). *Understanding by design* (2nd ed.). Alexandria, VA: ASCD.

Related Resources

At the time of publication, the following ASCD resources were available (ASCD stock numbers appear in parentheses). For up-to-date information about ASCD resources, go to www.ascd.org. You can search the complete archives of *Educational Leadership* at http://www.ascd.org/el.

ASCD EDge®
Exchange ideas and connect with other educators interested in differentiated instruction on the social networking site ASCD EDge at http://ascdedge.ascd.org.

Print Products
Assessment and Student Success in a Differentiated Classroom by Carol Ann Tomlinson and Tonya R. Moon (#108028)
The Differentiated Classroom: Responding to the Needs of All Learners (2nd ed.) by Carol Ann Tomlinson (#108029)
Leading and Managing a Differentiated Classroom by Carol Ann Tomlinson and Marcia B. Imbeau (#108011)

ASCD PD Online® Courses
Differentiated Instruction: Creating an Environment That Supports Learning (#PD11OC118)
Differentiated Instruction: Teaching with Student Differences in Mind (#PD11OC138)

For more information send e-mail to member@ascd.org; call 1-800-933-2723 or 703-578-9600, press 2; send a fax to 703-575-5400; or write to Information Services, ASCD, 1703 N. Beauregard St., Alexandria, VA 22311-1714 USA.

About the Authors

Carol Ann Tomlinson is William Clay Parrish, Jr. Professor, Chair of Educational Leadership, Foundations and Policy, and Co-director of the Institutes on Academic Diversity at the Curry School of Education, University of Virginia. Her university career follows a 20-year career as a public school teacher and a leader of district programs for both struggling and advanced learners. She and her colleagues developed a model for what we now call differentiated instruction in their work with heterogeneous 7th grade classrooms. Tomlinson was Virginia's Teacher of the Year in 1974 and won an All-University Teaching Award in 1994. The author of more than 300 publications, she works throughout the United States and internationally with educators who want to create classrooms that are more responsive to a broad range of learners.

Marcia B. Imbeau is a professor in the Department of Curriculum and Instruction at the University of Arkansas at Fayetteville, where she teaches graduate courses in two programs. She is actively involved in university and public school partnerships, working as a university liaison and teaching courses in curriculum development, differentiation, classroom management, and action research. Imbeau is a regular presenter at ASCD's annual conference and has worked with a variety of school districts' implementation efforts as a member of the ASCD's Differentiated Instruction Cadre. She is co-author (with Tomlinson) of *Leading and Managing a Differentiated Classroom,* along with several book chapters on the differentiated instruction and classroom management.

WHAT KEEPS YOU UP AT NIGHT?

ASCD Arias begin with a burning question and then provide the answers you need today—in a convenient format you can read in one sitting and immediately put into practice. Available in both print and digital editions.

arias

THE 5-MINUTE TEACHER

FOSTERING GRIT

Thomas R. HOERR

GRADING AND GROUP WORK

BROOK

TEACHING WITH TABLETS

Nancy FREY Douglas FISHER Alex GONZALEZ

Answers You Need
from Voices You Trust

ASCD | arias™